MW00711821

"Eli Ez
wisdom o
bring dai
kind. Pray... ,

poetry of sacred scripture with down-to-earth messages for each day's march. It can have special meaning for the doubter seeking a return to faith. Anybody in Twelve-Step recovery should find it highly effective as an inspirational guide."

—Mel B.
author of *New Wine, Walk in Dry Places,* and
Ebby: The Man Who Sponsored Bill W.

"*Praying for Recovery* is an excellent resource for recovering persons in all the Twelve-Step fellowships. Eli Ezry has distilled the powerful spiritual wisdom of Psalms and combined that with inspired, honest and moving personal reflections of a recovering addict. I think *Praying for Recovery* will be a useful tool for those seeking a pathway to balanced and sober spirituality. I would recommend it."

—Rabbi Sheila Peltz Weinberg
Jewish Community of Amherst
author of "Toward a Faith That Works: Overcoming Addictions," in *Worlds of Jewish Prayer*

"With the pen of a poet, Eli Ezry takes the words of the psalmist and brings them down to the depth of his personal experience of addiction, while at the same time, raising our spirits heavenward. These are words of beauty and of pain, words of hope and renewal."

—**Rabbi Kerry Olitzky**
coauthor of *Twelve Jewish Steps to Recovery* and
*Renewed Each Day: Daily
Twelve-Step Recovery Meditations Based on the Bible*

"Many Jews in Twelve-Step programs have been alienated by meetings in churches where the format seems Christian, and are seeking sources within Judaism to make the steps more familiar. This book offers them a valuable resource. I will give this book to every Jewish person I know who is in recovery; I believe they will recognize themselves and find hope."

—**Marcia Cohn Spiegel**
founder of the Alcoholism/Drug Action Program of
Jewish Family Service, Los Angeles
author of *The Heritage of Noah: Alcoholism in the
Jewish Community Today*

PRAYING
FOR
RECOVERY

PSALMS AND MEDITATIONS

Eli Ezry

SIMCHA
PRESS

An Imprint of Health Communications, Inc.

Deerfield Beach, Florida
www.simchapress.com

Library of Congress Cataloging-in-Publication Data

Ezry, Eli, date.
    Praying for recovery : psalms and meditations / Eli Ezry.
      p. cm.
    Includes bibliographical references and index.
    ISBN 1-55874-788-5 (trade paper)
    1. Twelve-step programs—Meditations. 2. Bible. O.T. Psalms—
Meditations. 3. Ezry, Eli, date. I. Title

  BL624.5 .E77 2000
  291.4'32—dc 21

                                  99-088436

©2000 Eli Ezry
ISBN 1-55874-788-5

Publisher: Simcha Press
          An Imprint of Health Communications, Inc.
          3201 S.W. 15th Street
          Deerfield Beach, Florida 33442–8190

Cover design by Andrea Perrine Brower
Inside book design by Dawn Grove

This book is dedicated to the men and women
of Twelve-Step fellowships everywhere, whose
courage, faith, wisdom and hope
are a constant source of inspiration.

Recognizing that anonymity
is the spiritual foundation
of all Twelve-Step traditions,
I have chosen to publish this book
under the pseudonym Eli Ezry.
In Hebrew, it means "my God is my help."

Weeping may stay through the night,
but in the morning, comes joy.

—Ps. 30:5

You have tried us, O God,
refining us, as silver is refined.
We came through fire and water
and You brought us out to
*   abundance.*

—Ps. 66:10, 12

We have escaped as a bird from the
*   fowlers' snare;*
the snare is broken, and we have
*   escaped!*

—Ps. 124:7–8

CONTENTS

THE TWELVE STEPS OF
ALCOHOLICS ANONYMOUS

1. We admitted we were powerless over alcohol—
   that our lives had become unmanageable.
2. Came to believe that a Power greater than ourselves could restore us to sanity.
3. Made a decision to turn our will and our lives
   over to the care of God as we understood Him.
4. Made a searching and fearless moral inventory
   of ourselves.
5. Admitted to God, to ourselves, and to another
   human being the exact nature of our wrongs.
6. Were entirely ready to have God remove all
   these defects of character.
7. Humbly asked Him to remove our shortcomings.
8. Made a list of all persons we had harmed, and
   became willing to make amends to them all.
9. Made direct amends to such people wherever
   possible, except when to do so would injure
   them or others.

10. Continued to take personal inventory and when we were wrong promptly admitted it.

11. Sought through prayer and meditation to improve our conscious contact with God as we understood Him, praying only for knowledge of His will for us and the power to carry that out.

12. Having had a spiritual awakening as the result of these Steps, we tried to carry this message to alcoholics, and to practice these principles in all our affairs.

WHY I WROTE THIS BOOK

It has been said that all addiction is a search for God, though addicts unfortunately search in the wrong places—whether in alcohol, drugs, gambling, food, pornography or work, or in another person, through codependency, sex or love. In order to recover from addiction, addicts must learn to search elsewhere for their Higher Power.

Many recovering addicts, however, have difficulties with prayer and traditional notions of God. For some, childhood experiences of religious communities and leaders have left them feeling alienated from organized religion. At the same time, they are learning in Twelve-Step programs that in order to ground themselves and find the spiritual center from which their recovery can grow, they need to cultivate their spirituality. Others, who may have strong religious beliefs, presently often feel alienated from God. Feeling guilty about the harm they caused themselves and others during their active addiction, newly recovering addicts can all too easily shy away from contact with their Higher Power at a time when it is crucial to reopen those channels of communication. This book is dedicated to helping all recovering addicts find and deepen a connection to their Higher Power, however they define it, whether they are confirmed believers or not-yet-believers looking for a new spiritual path.

I'd like to say a few words about how I came to write this book. I wrote it when I came into recovery for the second time. In my previous encounter with a Twelve-Step program I had not adequately used the basic tools of recovery. In over two years, I did not find a sponsor; only rarely did I draw on the support of others in the program outside the meeting rooms, and I never got beyond my doubts in the existence of a Higher Power to draw on prayer and meditation as aids to recovery. I tried to recover by my will alone, and as anyone who has recovered from addiction will tell you, that is simply not possible. The will of the addict is stronger than the unaided will of the recovering person. Inevitably, I went back to my old ways, causing great pain and humiliation to myself, my family and those who had put their trust in me.

The second time around I was determined to make the recovery program stick—and I knew that to do so, I had to make it my own. This book represents my efforts in learning to pray for recovery. The idea of a personal God was to me a remote and somewhat alien concept. For me, as for so many Jews of my generation, the biblical God in whom we were taught to believe as children was shattered by what I had learned of the Nazis' destruction of Europe's Jews. I came to see, though, that I had to get beyond this block to recover from addiction and save my life from the degradation into which it had sunk. I had to learn to pray with a full and open heart, even if I did not know to whom or to what force I was addressing my prayers.

Before then I had said many prayers, but as a lifelong agnostic I had little experience in really talking and listening to God. The biblical psalmists, I found, had come before me to show me the path they had walked. When I had no words of my own, I could try on their words and their wisdom. When I had to learn the vocabulary of gratitude, they reminded me how much I had to be grateful for. Their feelings of anguish and exaltation, their affirmations and their doubts—all were relevant to the journey I was taking. The psalmists gave me strength, courage and hope. Through their example, I learned to pray for my own recovery.

Just as I joined my prayer experiences to those of the psalmists, so I invite readers to build their own experiences of prayer upon the psalms and meditations I present in this book. There is an important saying in the Twelve-Step movement: "Place principles before personalities."

While these meditations began as personal reflections, they are more importantly a distillation of wisdom that came to me through the Twelve-Step program. They correlate the words of the Psalms with each of the Twelve Steps and with the spiritual work that particular step entails for recovering addicts. *Praying for Recovery* can be used either by those "working" the Twelve Steps for the first time, or by those who continue to revisit individual steps as part of their ongoing recovery. The index also points readers to specific concerns that they may wish to address in their prayers.

The early passages in the book are intended to help us acknowledge our suffering as addicts. Having accepted ourselves as addicts, we still need to understand and cope with our painful withdrawal from active addiction. As we face the spiritual and emotional challenges of living without addiction, we need to develop alternate ways of being in the world. One of these is a commitment, new to many of us, to daily contact with a Higher Power. Through this contact, modeled in the selections from Psalms and in the book's contemporary prayers, we can experience important goals of the recovery process firsthand: a lifelong learning about ourselves and a spiritual awakening that gradually allows us to share the blessings and promises of emotional sobriety with others.

My hope has been to keep this book from being a narrow prescription for how to pray for recovery. I have tried to leave as open as possible the mystery of how Spirit works in my life and in the collective life of the recovering community. Having learned to experience the presence and direction of my Higher Power through praying the Psalms, I am very clear that this contact has brought me many wonderful gifts. In sharing the gifts of strength and hope that I have gained through making the words of the Psalms my own, I hope to make it easier for others to see recovery as the spiritual path it is.

Step One

We admitted we were powerless over our addictive behavior—that our lives had become unmanageable.

My Life Has Become Unmanageable

I am drowning in the muddy slime,
and there is no foothold;
I have waded into the watery deep,
and the flood sweeps over me.
I am wearied with calling;
my throat is parched.

—Ps. 69:3–4

For the longest time, I could live in my addiction and seem to manage my life. But now that is no longer possible. The addiction has overwhelmed me and I might as well be drowning.

I pursued my drug of choice without any regard to the consequences for me or for others. Even after I began to experience negative consequences, I persisted. But now the costs are too great to bear any longer. My addictive compulsions have finally cost me respect in my eyes and in the eyes of others.

The chaos now reigning in my life is more than I can manage. I want to rejoin those whose lives make sense. But where do I begin? I am powerless over my addiction. If I do not get help soon, it will surely destroy me.

My Isolation as an Addict

You have put me in the lowest pit,
in dark places, in the depths.
You have distanced my friends from
*   me;*
You have made me abhorrent to them;
I am imprisoned and do not go out.

—Ps. 88:7, 9

I feel utterly alone. My shame is so great that I cannot share my secret life as an addict with anyone. When I am with others, I am only half present. I have cut them off from the reality of my life.

I suppose I am lying in the bed I made. And it feels as narrow as the grave. For there is no one to share this hell with me. All my relationships have been strained to the breaking point. Can any ray of light penetrate this darkness?

I realize that only in a Twelve-Step meeting is it safe for me to share my secret life. This thought does not take away the pain I feel, but it gives me the glimmer of hope I need today to survive.

Alone in My Withdrawal

I am like a vulture of the wilderness,
like an owl of the waste places.
I lie awake,
like a lonely bird on a rooftop.
My bread is ashes,
and I mingle tears with my drink.

—Ps. 102:7–8, 10

For so long, all I have known is my addiction. When lonely, I have resorted to it. When frustrated or irritable, when angry, tired, or hungry, I have always found a solution in my addictive behavior. Even when I wanted to celebrate, my addiction could keep me company. I could have a party all by myself.

Now that I am not acting out my compulsions, I am alone in a new way. My lifelong companion, my addiction, is not by my side, and I'm feeling how truly lonely and vulnerable I am. This new loneliness is so painful. I can feel in my body the old cravings, and I know what would bring relief. But I also am learning how temporary and how shame-filled that relief would be. I can't go back to who I've been. But who am I now? I'm crawling inside my own skin.

I desperately want to break out of this isolation. I will go to a meeting and find other recovering addicts who know the same struggles. There, I can at least share the pain I'm going through today.

How Can I Endure This Pain?

I am greatly bent and bowed down;
all day I walk about in a deep
  darkness.
I have grown numb, am utterly crushed;
I can only roar because of the turmoil
  in my heart.
My heart gasps, my strength has left
  me;
the light of my eyes is gone.

—Ps. 38:7, 9, 11

This has to be the hardest trial of my life. My energy is utterly drained. How can I survive without what I've used for so long to medicate my feelings?

My thoughts are all so self-abusive. They say, "I am defective. I am a worthless piece of junk. I am an immoral, incorrigible human being." I know I've done much that has been deceitful and callous, hurtful to myself and others. Right now, though, I can't focus on all the wrongs I've done. There will be time for that. My own wounds are crying out for healing.

I've been told that I am powerless to save myself. Will someone show me the way to recover from this dis-ease, which I've felt so much of my life?

Step Two

Came to believe that a Power greater than ourselves could restore us to sanity.

A Power Greater than Myself

In my complacency, I said,
"I shall never be shaken."
Sustaining Spirit, when it pleased You,
You stood me up as a mighty mountain.
But when You hid Your face, I was
  confounded.

—Ps. 30:7–8

I thought of myself as Mr. Invulnerable when acting out in my addiction—a Master of the Universe, the sort of person to whom other people's rules don't apply. "I'm entitled," I said, "after all I've put up with. Why shouldn't I do whatever I want—whatever makes me feel good? Who's stopping me? It's a free country."

That familiar ground is not so familiar

anymore. What had long seemed firm is quaking. And what I had assumed is all wrong. My life is not in my power to control or sustain. When I hit bottom in my addictive free-fall, by some miracle my life didn't end. I was able to reach out, to ask for healing and receive it. What has happened to me is enough to help me believe that there is a Power greater than myself, a Power that can save me from myself.

Higher Power, I need Your grace. Help me to find in You all the comfort I found in my addiction. Help me to stay open to experiencing Your grace today and every day. I pledge that I will never again take a single day of life for granted. My whole life, one day at a time, will be a song of gratitude.

Restored to Sanity

How precious is Your lovingkindness,
  God.
Human beings shelter in the shadow of
  Your wings.
They feast on the abundance of Your
  house,
and You give them drink from Your
  stream of delights.
For with You is the fountain of life;
By Your light, we see light.

                              —Ps. 36:8–10

As an addict, I've known the allure of
temptation: lying on my bed in the night,
fantasizing how I could next be satisfied,
recalling the thrills of past exploits and the
stolen pleasures they gave. Until now, I

have been powerless to resist such thoughts, feeling myself at their mercy whenever they arose. I never admitted the addiction's power over me, though, until I experienced the guilty terror of being found out, the shame of being exposed and thrown down.

Only from the bottom could I finally see a path climbing upward, a universe wider than the narrow horizon of my addiction, an order to creation, a guiding spirit deep in the nature of things that wants me and all of us recovering addicts to live sane and productive lives. A Higher Power accepts me as I am right now. And it is this love and total acceptance that feeds me when I share the fellowship of other recovering addicts. By accepting the gift of this love and turning it toward self-acceptance, I can begin over again.

I am not a worthless creature, but a God-inspired human who can contribute to the well-being of others. Led by my Higher Power, I can at last embark on the path of my true aspirations, upward toward the light. I see myself surrounded, enveloped by this light. This light is Yours, shining in the darkness as in the day.

Two Paths

Fortunate is the person
who no longer follows the counsel of
*   the wicked,*
nor takes the path of sinners,
nor sits among the insolent,
but delights in the teaching of the
*   Ever-Present,*
meditating on that teaching day and
*   night.*

—Ps. 1:1–2

Insanity, I have learned, is doing the same thing over and over while expecting different results. That's how I lived my life as an addict. I knew my actions jeopardized relationships I deeply valued, yet I kept on with those actions. In my insanity,

I thought I could live comfortably in two radically different worlds. One was a world of disorder and dark secrets, impulsive actions and emotional chaos—all of this for the thrill of a momentary high. The other was my orderly, presentable life: the respectable face I put on to meet all the other respectable faces around me. To live in that second world, though, I had to deny the existence of the first. I lied to myself and others to avoid facing the reality of my divided life as an addict.

My two worlds can no longer coexist. As a person who has suddenly become sane, I understand that if I keep doing the things I've been doing addictively for so long, I will continue to experience broken relationships and lost opportunities. As a newly sane person, I see that there really are two distinct paths for me.

One is the path I've been following. It leads only to death and destruction. The other is the path of living truthfully, accepting the reality of my life, however much it hurts to see who I've been. If I take the first step, You, Higher Power, will help me take the next. Help me to become deeply rooted in truthfulness and integrity, growing in faith and good works every day of my life.

A World in Proportion

Your trees drink their fill,
the cedars of Lebanon that you planted;
birds make their nests in them,
the stork—the fir trees are her home.
The high mountains are for wild goats;
the rocks, a refuge for badgers.

—Ps. 104:16–18

I am not at the center of this world. I am one of myriad creatures, all part of the sacred web of life. No one is so isolated that his or her life does not touch another's. As a small but integral part of Your creation, I know that my nature is fundamentally good. I can realize my goodness, which is integral to that design, by living in harmony with my surroundings, or I can disrupt it by acting unthinkingly and selfishly.

That's what I've done in my addiction. I created havoc in the world around me by giving free rein to my appetites and my emotions—to the unthinking, impulsive forces within me—and shortchanging my spiritual nature. By losing a sense of proportion, I disrupted the balance of elements within me and within all the lives that I touched.

As I meditate on the design of creation, I pray for the ability to restore that balance within me. By living a life at peace with myself, I trust that I will come to live at peace with all the world. I bless You, Higher Power, for my growing awareness that the goodness in my life is integrally connected to the sacred web of life around me. For all that I have today, I am deeply grateful.

Step Three

Made a decision to turn our will
and our lives over to the care
of God, as we understood
God.

The House That Recovery Builds

If the Builder does not build the house,
then those who build it labor in vain;
if the Watcher does not watch over the
*   city,*
then the night watch stays up in vain.
In vain your rising early, your staying
*   up late,*
you who eat the bread of anxious toil.
For God provides for you, loved ones,
*   while you sleep.*

—Ps. 127:1–2

I have lived for a long time in the house that addiction built, a house whose foundation is anxiety and manipulation, secrecy and deceit. In the house of addiction, I erected thick walls between me and other people. Between me and my own feelings of fear, anger and shame, the walls are even thicker. Whenever I've needed an escape from those uncomfortable feelings, I have hidden behind the walls of my addiction.

It took a long time for me to admit that I could no longer live in the house that addiction built. I can now also admit that I do not know how to build a different kind of house. I sense that I have within me the capacity for a higher, better self, but I know that I am powerless to cultivate that self on my own. I need You, Higher Power, to teach me new strategies for living.

I trust that You, as the one true Builder, will teach me how to build a house I can live in, a house built on a foundation of integrity and honesty. With that foundation, I can at last surrender my unaided will to You. I can have faith that what happens to me today is for my highest good.

Accepting Vulnerability

*Hear my voice, Ever-Present, when
    I call;
be gracious to me and answer me.
My heart has said, in Your name,
    "Seek my face";
Infinite Source, I do seek Your face.
Show me Your way, Great Teacher,
and lead me on a level path,
because of my ever-alert enemies.*

—Ps. 27:7–8, 11

It sometimes seems that I'm in a battle
zone. People object to the way I do this or
that. They mistake my motives and criticize
me, often harshly. But I am my harshest
critic. I put myself down all day long. My
negative thoughts are internal enemies,

destroying my peace of mind. I fear others' hostile reactions to me, and I fear my own vengeful thoughts that arise in reaction to them.

Free me, Higher Power, from this recurrent fear. At this vulnerable moment, help me to feel accepted just as I am. I rely on the certainty that You are available to me at every moment for prayer or meditation. Do not disappoint me now by failing to make Your spirit known to me.

Connecting with You, I see that I am not better or worse than others, because Your way equalizes everyone. It is a straight and level path between extremes. I trust in the goodness that comes from walking that path with You. I want to teach others what I know today: only our Higher Power can give us a hope that never fails.

Being Led

Guiding Spirit, You are my shepherd;
I lack nothing.
You lay me down in grassy pastures;
You lead me to rest beside tranquil
  waters.
You refresh my soul;
You direct me in paths of right living,
because of who You are.

—Ps. 23:1–3

I acknowledge that I am not a good guide for myself, having lived a life that was often out of control. So every day I let myself be guided as I walk with my Shepherd. My Shepherd makes sure that I pasture in a place with plenty of grass and running water. Left to my own devices, I might wander away and break my neck in a dangerous gorge. If something wild threatens, my Shepherd's watchful eye and stick protect me and keep me safe with the flock. Every time I look toward my Shepherd, I breathe a sigh of relief, because I know I have everything I need.

Working with a sponsor in my Twelve-Step program has prepared me for this walk with You, Higher Power. Having taken this journey before me, my sponsor can point me where to go and where to avoid. And with You by my side, I know that I'm on the path of living right, one step, one day at a time. I have so much to learn—so many feelings that I'm conscious of for what seems like the first time. As I accept my vulnerability, walking alongside You helps me to feel safe. Each day, as I have fears, I can set them aside and begin to trust that Your goodness can come to me without my having to deserve it, without my having to earn everything on my own.

I look around and experience so many blessings. Life is indeed a bountiful feast. I no longer define myself by what I lack or by focusing on those who prevent me from getting what I need. I have everything I need and trust that I will have everything I need in the future. My only prayer is for right intention: that I may continue to walk with You as long as You grant me life.

Surrendering Temptation

Set a guard, Protector, over my mouth;
keep watch at the threshold of my lips.
Let my heart not turn to anything bad,
becoming embroiled in wicked deeds,
with people who do evil;
let me not partake of their delicacies.

—Ps. 141:3–4

Temptation beckons many times a day, sometimes teasing me, sometimes stalking. Just a little hit, it offers. Fantasies come unbidden and unseen. I am powerless over these temptations. My mind and my heart easily succumb, and I fall into the well-known ruts of the addiction. I open my mouth and the addict in me speaks words that I no longer want to hear myself saying. One more misstep, and I am on the way to a full-blown relapse.

I am an easy mark for temptations—unless I surrender them all to You. Surrendering means letting You, rather than my inner addict, teach me how to respond. I hear You tell me to stay away from the people, places and things that occupied me during my active addiction. Today, I do stay away. Today, I am blessed to have new companions, new thoughts, new prayers.

Today I pray, Higher Power, for the courage and wisdom to keep surrendering these temptations to You, so I can honor my commitment to recovery as a total way of life. Let me not slip back into the huge gaping hole that is my addiction. Help me keep this prayer on my lips as I become ever more used to serving You.

As We Understand God

*Enlightener, You open the eyes of the
  blind.*
*Straightener, You lift up those who are
  bent down.*
Justice-Lover, You love the righteous.
Provider, You watch over the stranger.
*You give courage to the orphan and
  the widow,*
but the way of the wicked You thwart.

—Ps. 146:8–9

As best I can, I turn my life over to the
care of God, as I understand God. My
understanding of God is limited, though,
by my thoughts and experience. I am
tempted to see God as everything that
my addicted self is not: kind, unselfish,

compassionate, slow to anger. But I need to remember that all my definitions limit God. My prayer, Higher Power, is that I can let You be You and accept however You manifest Yourself in my life.

Rather than trying to understand how You work, it's best for me to stick to the things I do understand: I was a prisoner of my addiction, but today I am free from obsession. I was blind to my own problems, but today I see myself more clearly than ever before. I bottomed out in my own eyes and in the eyes of those around me, but today I can hold my head up. I hurt many people, myself included, but today I am following a path that is turning my life around. I lived a double life, estranged from myself and others, but today I attempt to live confidently and honestly, supported by the loving fellowship of my recovering community.

For all of this, I thank You, God. These blessings are as real as the air I breathe or the ground I walk on. Let this be enough understanding of You, Higher Power, for today.

Step Four

Made a searching and fearless
moral inventory of ourselves.

God Challenges Us

When you see a thief, you are pleased
  with him;
you partake with adulterers.
You loosen your mouth for evil,
and bind your tongue to deceit.
When you sit down, you slander your
  brother;
you defame your own mother's son.

—Ps. 50:18–20

Arrogance. Blasphemy. Character assassination. Debauchery—down through the alphabet of my vices. You, Higher Power, will hold me guilty for all the damage I've done, until I take up Your challenge to undertake a searching and fearless moral inventory. You are said to be compassionate

and merciful, but You extend Your mercy
only to those who go to all possible lengths
to turn their lives around. You do not look
lightly on those who say, "I'll repent today
and sin again tomorrow."

You and I know that much of the harm I
have done was caused by my addiction. We
both know that I did not create the condi-
tions in which the addiction developed. I
acknowledge, however, that it was I and no
other who continued in my pattern of
negative behaviors, no matter how they
started. Will I now become an adult and
take responsibility for my actions? Or will I
hesitate longer at the brink of this abyss?

I understand that when I undertake a
full moral accounting, a new phase in my
life begins. If I take this step with my
whole heart, mind and soul, it can be the
beginning of a meaningful life that we create together. I know You are ready. Am I?

Searching and Fearless

I acknowledge my transgressions,
am ever aware of my failings.
Indeed, You desire our inner truth,
so show me wisdom in my secret heart.
Create in me a pure heart, God,
and renew a firm spirit within me.

—Ps. 51:5, 8, 12

I pray for the courage to face the reality of my life. I cannot change the fact that I am an addict. I cannot change all the negative consequences that have resulted from my behaviors. What I can do is take up the challenge of looking fearlessly at myself. I see that I have been dominated by pride, fear and self-pity, by hidden and overt anger, by envy and resentment, often by lust and gluttony. I have not been who I could have been. Only by searching into all my inward parts can I reveal the truth about my life. And only that truth can begin to set me free.

To take this inventory, I must face up to my whole history. Until now, I have not been ready to go down to the basement storeroom labeled "Defective Parts," unlock the door and turn on the light. Until now, I have not wanted to sift through the many piles of mental and emotional junk I've thrown down there. Until now, I have not been willing to look closely at my character. But with You as a partner, Higher Power, I am no longer afraid of what I will find. I can now own the parts of myself that I have for so long disowned.

To stay with this daunting task, I ask You for the gifts of patience, discernment and a firm will. I ask for Your help and guidance to keep me focused on my own wrongdoings and not on the hurts I've suffered from others. So I can bring into the light what has been so long closed up and hidden, I ask for Your illumination. Only with these gifts can I sustain the searching and fearless moral inventory that You demand. Only if I see clearly who I have been can I discern the person You would like me to become. I place my trust in Your plan for cleaning up my soul. May it lead me, as it has led others before me, to find a new heart and a new spirit.

Unmasking Deceit

Why do you pride yourself on evil,
*   bold fellow,*
when God's lovingkindness is available
*   each day?*
Your tongue threatens calamity;
like a sharpened razor, it practices
*   deceit.*
You love evil more than good,
lies more than truthful speech.

—Ps. 52:3–5

I was that bold fellow, living a shameless life and lying about it. I lied because I could not stand to feel the shame that had led to my addiction. And I lied to cover up the shame of my behaviors that sustained it. I became a master of grandiose rationalizations.

I convinced myself that I was entitled to my sprees, that other people were to blame. As my thinking became distorted by my addictive desires, I lost touch with what was truly good and bad. I once knew what was good, but I became incapable of reaching for it.

I began to unmask this history of deceit and moral collapse when I came into the rooms of my Twelve-Step fellowship. Gingerly, I began to tell the story of my double life as an addict, a life rooted in deceiving others and myself. As I heard others being honest, gradually I came clean with more and more of what I had done, lessening my shame by naming it.

But outside the rooms, I still practiced my cover-up. I feared exposure and shaming. As I undertake this moral inventory and shine a searchlight on my own dishonesty, I recognize that I am also capable of a new, rigorous honesty. Thank You, Higher Power, for the courage that allows me to see myself more and more honestly. May the day come when honesty is as natural to me as breathing.

What Are My Good Qualities?

Holy One, who may stay in Your tent?
Who may dwell upon Your holy
*   mountain?*
A person who walks with integrity,
does what is right, and speaks the
*   heart's truth;*
Whoever acts in these ways shall
*   never be shaken.*

—Ps. 15:1–2, 5

I am overcome with remorse over all the ways I have acted wrongly. How can I begin the path of return to You if so much is expected of me? How can I leave behind the wrongs I did in the past and move on to create the present that I want and that You want for me?

In addition to taking an inventory of my wrongdoing, I can also acknowledge the good that I have done. Since I've embarked on recovery, many of my better qualities—especially compassion and generosity—have begun to come out of the shadows and into the light. What's more, I have found a place in my heart and mind for You, Higher Power.

For every negative quality that I have manifested in my addiction, let me pair it with an opposite, positive quality that I have glimpsed somewhere in my life. Help me to accept my character assets. With these strengths, I can begin to climb Your holy mountain. With Your help, I will be true to my best vision of myself and Your hopeful vision of me.

Step Five

Admitted to God, to ourselves and to another human being the exact nature of our wrongs.

The Exact Nature
of My Wrongs

O God, You know my folly;
my wrongs are not hidden from You.
You know my reproach,
my shame and my disgrace;
all my adversaries are arrayed before
    You.

—Ps. 69:6, 20

I have been told in my Twelve-Step fellowship that a full confession is the next step I need to take. My tears show me how vulnerable I feel. I am full of trepidation at the thought of sharing my character faults and the details of my story with another.

Higher Power, you must already know

the exact nature and the full extent of my wrongs. Yet You have not turned away from me. Perhaps the person I've chosen to hear my story will accept me as You have done.

Be with me, Higher Power, in this difficult hour. Help me to tolerate whatever feelings arise in me. Grant me the wisdom to see and explain my wrongs with all the clarity I can muster. Help me to embrace the rigorous honesty that I need from myself and to which You challenge me.

Out of the Depths

Out of the depths I call to You,
  Redeemer.
Gracious One, hear my voice;
may Your ears be attentive
to the sound of my pleas.
My soul waits for You,
more eagerly than watchmen wait for
  the morning,
watchmen for the morning.

—Ps. 130:1–2, 6

Can I make the exact nature of my wrongs clear to myself, let alone to another? Will I be understood? And if understood, won't I be sternly judged? Look at all the harm I've done, all the damage I've caused. Wrestling with these thoughts and fears, I am pulled down into the murky depths, back into the dark night of my soul.

From the depths of my being, I cry out in pain. Feeling Your presence, hoping for Your answering word, I cry out Your name. It is a ladder on which I climb upward toward You. Patiently, I enumerate my wrongs, and rung by rung, I climb out of the depths to which my negative thinking has consigned me.

You will surely accept my confession with compassion and with love. Let me be filled today with that certainty.

To Be Known by God

Where could I go from Your spirit?
Where could I run from Your presence?
If I ascended to heaven, You'd be
    there!
If I made my bed in the Pit, You'd be
    there too!
If I flew upon the wings of the dawn,
and dwelt at the far reaches of the sea,
even there Your hand would be leading
    me,
Your right hand grasping mine.

—Ps. 139:7–10

So much of my life as an active addict
was based on keeping things hidden. I felt
secure in assuming that people would
never unearth my secrets. That false

security is gone. I know that what has been hidden must come to light. I know that I can be saved from who I've been only by bringing forth what's inside of me. And yet I am afraid to do so. To be so intimately known—to be known by God! What an awesome and fearful thought.

I breathe deeply and my fear dissipates. You know me intimately already. You have been my Intimate Companion since I took the first step toward You. You were my Intimate Companion before I had any awareness of You. So nothing I say today could surprise You. I can let You know everything about my past, everything about which I feel guilt and shame.

My story takes a long time to tell. When I am finished, I sense that something important has shifted inside me. Having shared my story with You, I feel my life more deeply connected to You and to everything around me—to all that is tied to you through the invisible bonds of Spirit. Let me become ever more conscious of my spiritual connection to You and of my place in Your larger scheme of things.

Forgiven

When I kept silent, my substance
*   wasted away,*
as I roared all day long.
So I acknowledged my sin to You,
and didn't hide my guilt,
saying, "I hereby confess my trans-
*   gressions to the Eternal."*
And You took away the guilt for my
*   sin.*

—Ps. 32:3, 5

From the vantage point of the fifth step,
I look back at the whole progress of my
addiction. I taste again the bittersweet
poison of addictive craving. I rehearse the
lies and feel the debilitating isolation of
having kept so much secret for so long. I

recall how unmanageable my life became, how agonizing the pain of my failed attempts to break my enslavement to addiction. Through all of this, I was utterly alone. The knowledge of that loneliness is still in my body. How constricted I felt having no one with whom to speak honestly of these things.

What a relief to come into the rooms of the Twelve-Step fellowship and give vent to my feelings! On that day, I rejoined the human community. Though I would never willingly choose to relive the pain of my addiction, I begin to be grateful for it. My suffering brought me to this sacred community and to You, Higher Power. You have given me a freedom that I never knew before—the freedom to choose how to live. I celebrate that freedom today. My addiction no longer controls my actions. I am a human being with flaws and with strengths, a human being who continues to make significant life-enhancing changes. I no longer need to dwell on the debasing details of my story. Letting go of them, I can begin to make room for the new self that is gradually emerging in recovery. I can now look back to my past for valuable lessons that I can take into the rest of my life.

What a blessing it is for me to speak with You, Higher Power, and to feel Your understanding, forgiving and guiding spirit. Thank You for the privilege of being known and loved by You. Coming from where I was, I see that my ongoing recovery is truly a miracle. Today I am filled with gratitude and joy.

Step Six

Were entirely ready to have God remove all these defects of character.

Step Seven

Humbly asked God to remove all our shortcomings.

Beyond Envy and Resentment

Seeing the well-being of the wicked,
I envied those boasters.
They suffer no pangs;
their bodies are healthy.
Not for them ordinary human toil;
they are not stricken along with us.

—Ps. 73:3–5

I sometimes envy those whose lives haven't been overturned by addiction. They haven't ruined their emotional or physical health, lost jobs, or broken up relationships and families. They have children or a partner at home, money in the bank and are singing all the way to the health spa. Envying their happiness—

about which I really know nothing—
allows me to feel sorry for myself. Instead
of indulging in envy, what I need to do at
such times is practice gratitude—"Thank
You, Higher Power, for all that you've
given me"—and then make a list of God's
gifts to me.

I know from experience that gratitude
counteracts envy. But can gratitude dis-
lodge a grudge that I've nourished with
resentment? The more I resent someone,
the more of my mental space that person
occupies. I replay unpleasant scenes; I
rehearse countless clever replies that I'll
never deliver. If I'm obsessing about what
someone did to me, I'm at risk of becoming
emotionally unsober again. Instead, I look
for the lesson that person's behavior offers
me. How is it like things I've done in the
past? How can I avoid doing to others what

that person has done to me? Accepting such lessons, I let go of my resentment and find yet another reason for gratitude.

Higher Power, I need to stop thinking about all the people I've envied and resented. Help me to detach from them. If they have harmed me in some way, help me to forgive them. And if I have harmed them and they are now angry at me, help me to see that it was my own actions that alienated me from them. Envy and resentment take me away from myself and make me a slave to others. I humbly ask You to remove my envy and resentment. I want to be free today. With Your help, I can be free.

Beyond Anger

Refrain from anger, and abandon rage;
  don't get enflamed:
it brings only harm.
Commit your way to the Pathfinder;
trust in God, and God will do what
  you need.

—Ps. 37:8, 5

Every day I become a little more conscious of how my unacknowledged anger
has shaped the way I act. Before having the
Twelve Steps as a guide, I went through life
unconscious about my anger, which came
out sideways, whether in criticism, irrita-
bility, procrastination or sarcasm. Only
when I exploded in rage did I realize how
angry I was. But by then it was too late to

prevent the ugly damage my rage inflicted on others.

So much of this pattern, I now see, goes back to old angers and resentments. I've heard it said that rage is resentment that has aged. I commit myself to finding a safe place to express all my old resentments. I will pass the anger back to where it came from so I no longer pass it on. If I become angry today, I will name my anger and pray to let it go. And if I need to take action, I will remain emotionally sober. I am no longer willing to shame another to feel better about myself. That would only perpetuate an endless cycle of anger and shame.

Higher Power, I need Your help in removing this load of built-up anger from where it has taken residence in my character. I hand this defect over to You, knowing that I am powerless to remove it without Your help. Prepare me so that I can fully commit myself to making the world safe for those who encounter me. I will begin by looking for You in the face of each person I meet. I know that You will show me the way.

Beyond Deceit

Remove from me the way of falsehood,
and grace me with Your teaching.
I choose the way of faithfulness;
Your rules agree with me.
Turn my eyes away from seeing vanity;
revive me through Your ways!

—Ps. 119:29–30, 37

I am sick of secrets and lies. They have turned to ashes in my mouth. I have glossed over uncomfortable truths to make myself look better than I am. I have lived a double life and lost my self-respect and the respect and trust of friends and loved ones. Your way, Higher Power, is a different way. I need to walk on Your path, with new companions, following Your wisdom as I've learned it in my Twelve-Step program.

So today I pray for the willingness to have You entirely remove all forms of deceit from my character. And I make these affirmations: Today, I am willing to stop being secretive. I ask for Your help in learning to be appropriately open about myself. Today, I am willing to stop being unreliable. I ask for Your help in learning to be reliable and truthful in all my dealings. Today, I am willing to stop being dishonest. I ask for Your help in learning to be honest with myself and others.

May the power of the honesty for which I am striving carry me toward ever greater truthfulness in all areas of my life. May it be Your will, Higher Power, to make me a vehicle for spreading truth and honesty wherever I go.

Beyond Arrogance

*Eternal, my heart is no longer raised
    high,
nor my eyes lifted up.
I am no longer concerned with things
    too great
or too far beyond me.
Have I not composed and quieted my
    soul?*

—Ps. 131:1–2

For the longest time, my life was dominated by insecurity. I feared life, so I fanta-
sized and lived in my addiction. My
reveries took me back into the past or forward into the future. But the art of recovery, I am learning, is to accept reality today.
I do accept my reality today. I am

focused on tasks that I can reasonably hope to accomplish. I need neither the highs that substances give nor the lurid or grandiose fantasies that once fed my addiction and falsely quelled my insecurity.

If I take undue credit for this progress, I know that my recovery can easily be jeopardized. So I ask Your help now in removing my prideful character defects. I beg of You: Remove all trace of arrogance and grandiosity from my character and help me practice humility. Remove the self-indulgence that permitted my addiction to flourish and help me practice strict discipline. Remove my self-centeredness, Higher Power, and help me practice self-awareness.

As I become willing with Your help to let these character defects die in me, so may You breathe new life into my character assets, so that they may live and thrive.

Step Eight

Made a list of all persons we had
harmed and became willing to
make amends to them all.

Step Nine

Made direct amends to such
people wherever possible,
except when to do so would
injure them or others.

Counting Each Day

*Seventy are the years of our life,
or, if we are strong, eighty,
but pride in our years is weari-
    some and vain;
quickly cut off, we fly away.
So teach us to count our days
that we may bring forth a heart
    of wisdom.*

—Ps. 90:10, 12

Many of those who were angered by my addictive behaviors have seen no reason to become forgiving. As I come to understand the hurt that started my addiction and that caused me to hurt others, I can empathize with their hurt. Understanding and regretting what I did, I want to communicate my remorse to those I have harmed. I realize that until I make my peace with them, my rehabilitation is far from complete.

The list of those I have harmed is long. It includes many near and dear to me. It also includes some who were no more than passing strangers, witting or unwitting accomplices to my addiction. All the names I can now list are laid out before You, Higher Power. I pray for the willingness to make direct amends to all those whom I have hurt. I pray for the courage to contact every person and for the wisdom to know what amends I need to make to each.

But what am I to do about those I can no longer reach or those whose names I never knew? Show me how my concern for the suffering of others can serve as an indirect amends to those I have harmed. Guide me to undertake service that will help me atone for what I have done. And teach me, Higher Power, all the ways I can amend my life, one day at a time, so each day truly counts. Let my whole life be an offering to You of those changes and choices I make on a daily basis. For all those I cannot reach, may this amends-making suffice.

Making Amends Through Faith

When my mind was embittered,
and my feelings enflamed,
I was ignorant, knowing nothing;
I acted like a beast toward You.
But now I am with You always;
You have grabbed onto my right hand.
You guide me with Your advice
and lead me toward honor.

—Ps. 73:21–24

So often, I have spoken lightly of God and spiritual things. I assumed the persona and philosophy of a cynic. The only thing real to me was what I could see. I allowed my agnosticism—my lack of a certain knowledge about God—to harden into unbelief. I said, "God is only a game of words." I took my finite perspective as the only measure of reality.

As I played those mental games, I allowed myself to drift away from the certainty of my childhood connection with You, Higher Power. Today, I need no more certainty than my knowledge that You are my guiding and indwelling spirit.

As I return to You and turn my heart and will to Your service, may I correct the harm that my cavalier cynicism and illusions caused in Your world. I know that if I keep You ever in my thoughts, I will live each day honorably. May this be Your will.

Paying Back

What can I give back to You, Bountiful
  One,
for all the benefits I have received?
I lift up this cup of deliverance
and call on Your name, Powerful One.
I hereby pay my vows to You, Deliverer,
in the presence of all Your people.

—Ps. 116:12–14

I owe so much to You, Higher Power. You restored me to a life that is worth living. Keep me alive so that I can begin to repay the debt I owe. For in giving me this step of making amends, You offer me the chance to repair what I have marred, to rebuild what I have torn down. I can make appropriate restitution to people I have harmed, put the past behind me and start today with a clean slate.

In harming others, I also defaced and diminished Your image in them. When I now see You in the faces of people I meet and treat them with the respect they deserve, I am conscious of repairing the breaches I caused through disrespecting others. When I freely make a choice for recovery rather than for addiction and compulsion, I am conscious of not causing any further harm. This, too, is a way that I can pay back my debt to You for the life You have restored to me.

Thank you for Your compassion that allows me to begin over again each day.

Turning Toward Hope

Why so bowed down, my soul?
Why such turmoil inside me?
Hope in God!
I will yet offer thanks
to my Deliverer, my God.

—Ps. 42:6

My addiction exiled me from myself. I am a person with great potential for love and awareness of how to serve others. And yet for many years, I resented other people's claims upon me while freely servicing my addictive needs. How am I to make amends to myself for depriving me of so much of life's goodness? How am I to make amends to myself for not living up to my potential?

I have spent too many days feeling sorry for myself, getting teary-eyed on the phone or in front of the mirror. Why so downcast? Why is it so hard to let go of the past? All I have is today. I can wonder at the miracle of a tree, marvel at all living creatures and remember that I, too, have within me the force of my Higher Power. How can I let that divine spark languish in self-pity?

I shall make amends. I commit myself to taking care of me, body and soul. As I am loved by You, Higher Power, so will I love myself and be good to myself. I will continue to keep regular hours for work and sleep. I'll exercise and eat healthy foods. I'll allocate time for recreation, both with others and when alone. I will continue to cultivate my self-awareness by honestly talking to friends and writing in my journal, and I will always find time to pray and to meditate. For I know that in talking to You, whether with words or in silence, when I empty myself of all else, I fill up with the joy and knowledge of You.

Direct Amends

I lift my eyes to the mountains:
Where does my help come from?
My help comes from You, Near One,
Maker of sky and land.
You will not let my foot slip;
You will not doze while watching over
    me.

—Ps. 121:1–3

It is time for me to make direct amends to someone that I have deeply wronged. I am not taking this step so that this person will forgive me or like me again. I am doing it because it is the right thing for me to do. I cannot go forward unless I clean up my past.

Yet this person could easily reject my amends and push me away. This thought fills me with fear. Be with me, Higher Power, in this moment of deep vulnerability. When I pick up the phone to make the appointment, when I ring the doorbell and walk through the door, when I see again the face of the person whom I hurt, help me to feel Your watchful presence enveloping me, protecting me. Help me to muster the courage I need to walk through that door.

In making my amends, I could easily become manipulative. So help me to stay focused on my own wrongs, not on what this person might or might not think of me. With You by my side, my foot will not slip. I am ready. Teach me what I have to learn.

Step Ten

Continued to take personal
inventory, and when we were
wrong promptly admitted it.

God Takes Our Inventory

*Who may ascend the mountain of the
    Incorruptible?*
*And who may stand up in My holy
    place?*
*A person with clean hands and a pure
    heart,*
*who neither takes false oaths by My
    life,*
nor swears deceitfully.
*That one will bear blessings from the
    Source of All,*
vindication from God, who saves.

—Ps. 24:3–5

Sadly, I have lived much of my life
unconsciously. Every day, in order to live a
more conscious life, I must ask myself

questions about my behavior. I need to
take note of where I have fallen short of
my ideals, while neither burdening myself
with harsh self-judgment nor letting myself
off the hook by making light of my shortcomings. So I ask myself:

In what ways have I put myself first,
ignoring others' legitimate needs? Have I
been too easily offended when I could have
shown understanding? Have I used my
power over others constructively or arro-
gantly? Have I acted kindly toward others
because I cared about them or because I
wanted to think well of myself? Have I
done anything that either intentionally or
unintentionally hurt another? Did I slight
another, causing hurt feelings? Did I speak
in anger when I could have shown compassion? Was I rigid when I could have
been flexible, irritable when I could have

let go? Did I nourish any resentments, whether secretly or openly? Have I denigrated others behind their backs, damaging their reputations?

How honest have I been with myself and others in my personal and business dealings? Did I lie or shave the truth in order to make myself look better? Have I been conscious about the motives behind my actions? Have I been as open about them as I could reasonably be? And what of my commitments to myself to live as fully as possible? Was I timid when I could have spoken up? Did I act helplessly when I could have taken responsibility? Did I pity myself when I could have stood in my power? Was I needy and insecure when I could have been secure in the knowledge of Your loving support, Higher Power? Did I take time to seek Your help today?

Higher Power, thank You for Your concern about my character. And thank You for seeing me in ways that increase my vigilance and my honesty. The tenth step keeps me honest. Let me stay in the habit of making an honest inventory every day. And let me get in the habit of not waiting until tomorrow to admit that I was wrong today. For all I have is today.

Hidden Flaws

Errors—who can discern them?
Cleanse me of hidden flaws.
Restrain Your servant also from willful
sins;
let them not rule over me.
Then I shall be sound,
cleansed of great transgression.

—Ps. 19:13–14

It seems almost every day I find another reason to update my personal inventory. Part of me wants to say, "Enough with character defects already! Aren't I just perpetuating the false thinking that I'm defective?" But another part of me answers, "I'm not defective as a person. But, given my long conditioning as an addict, my actions are inevitably going to reveal flaws in my character. As long as those flaws remain hidden, I can't work on them." So help me, Higher Power, to bring my hidden flaws to light. And as they come to light, I will continue to ask for Your help in removing them.

I know I'm going to make mistakes. These mistakes can be lessons for me, if I do not beat myself up about them. If I look at them as opportunities for growth, then I can bring my buried life more and more into consciousness. That is my only chance to erase the harmful patterns that have dominated my life. Grant me, Higher Power, the persistence I need for the hard work of looking at myself through the light of honesty and truth.

Doing Good

Expect good for the person who lends
*   graciously,*
who conducts all business equitably;
who gives freely to the poor,
whose righteousness is enduring—
that person's dignity will be exalted and
*   honored.*

—Ps. 112:5, 9

What good will I do today?

If yesterday I did not share my financial resources with those less fortunate than I, may I do so today. If yesterday I did not relieve another's suffering, if yesterday I did not speak out against injustice, if yesterday I did not smile at someone who needed encouragement, if yesterday I did not offer someone loving support, if yesterday I did not laugh at my own foibles, if yesterday I did not praise God—let me do so today.

Let me not go through my days wrapped up in my own little world. Let me always find opportunities to bring more light and love into the world, for that, I know, is Your will, Higher Power, the end for which we were created.

Staying Away

*I neither keep company with the
   frivolous,
nor seek out those who live double
   lives.
I wash my hands in innocence
and circle Your altar, Life-Giver,
making my voice heard in thanksgiving
and telling of all Your wonders.*

—Ps. 26:4, 6–8

Let me enumerate all the things I used
to do that I no longer do today.

Let me remember all the people with
whom I was up to no good who are no
longer in my life today.

Let me recall all the places I used to
enter that I no longer enter today.

Thank You, Higher Power, for the willingness to recall where I came from and the path I took to find my way to You. Thank You for teaching me to take a daily inventory, helping me find the self-esteem that lets me look at my successes as well as at my failures. And thank You, above all else, for the new life You have granted me. May You keep me always aware of what I did in the past, of who I can be today and of how I can best serve You.

Step Eleven

Sought through prayer and meditation to improve our conscious contact with a Power greater than ourselves, praying only for knowledge of God's will for us and the power to carry that out.

But I Am a Stranger

Hear my prayer, Listener,
and attend to my plea;
Do not be silent in the face of my tears.
For I am a stranger with You,
a temporary resident, like all of my
*   ancestors.*

—Ps. 39:13

Sometimes it is so hard for me to begin this conversation with You. If I get out of the daily habit, I can easily forget who I'm talking to or what is appropriate for me to say. And even when I do speak, how do I know it's going to be a dialogue? It's so hard to know how to listen for Your answers, to discern exactly what is and what isn't a message from You. What's more, I sometimes have problems figuring out how I can address You at all. I am a human being and You are not. I am dying a little bit every day and You are not. Even if my soul lives after me, it is often hard for me to access that immortal part of me in the here and now. In the here and now, I am in pain. Everything I love will die. So what can I gain from talking to You?

I stop my complaining and allow myself to listen and wait. I empty my mind and recall one of Your teachings. Those who have learned from You advise people to carry in each of their two pockets a different slip of paper. On one is written, "I am but dust and ashes," and on the other, "For me, the world was created." Yes, I am a mortal being, mere "dust and ashes," a stranger to divinity. And yes, I am also a God-inspired creature. "The world was created for me" means that everything has been provided me so I can bring forth the image of God in myself and in others.

I need to hear both these messages. I need to keep a balanced perspective and not swing wildly toward either grandiosity or self-abasement. I am here at Your service. Teach me, Higher Power, how I can best serve.

Staying Put

I have wished, "O for the wings of a
　　dove!
I would fly away, then alight;
would wander far
and stay in the wilderness.
I would quickly find me a refuge
from the rushing wind and the storm."
I cast my burden on You, Comforter,
and You will sustain me.

　　　　　　　　　　　　　—Ps. 55:7–9, 23

Events in my life have shaken me. I fear what others think of me. And I want to run away from their judgments—anything to avoid a confrontation. Is that what I should do, Higher Power, flee rather than stand my ground?

Immediately I know Your answer. I am a human being who has the capacity to confront my fears. And I have learned that my fears are almost always generated by my own negative thinking rather than by anything outside me. "I am not good enough." That is the old message. No matter how much I try to drown it out, that voice continues to claim my attention. Any failure, any perceived inadequacy on my part brings it right back into my ear.

You whisper a different message to me. I don't need to succeed at any particular task in order to merit Your love. I am good enough—just as I am. I am accepted—for who I am. I belong—where I am. Indeed, I will stay put. I will not be so easily moved. Instead, I will walk with my fears, getting to know them till they frighten me no more. Thank You, Higher Power, for revealing Your will for me.

Feast or Famine?

O God, You are my God!
I rise early for You;
my soul thirsts for You;
my body faints with longing for You,
as in a land that is dry and faint
*   from no water.*
For in the sanctuary I have glimpsed
*   You,*
seen Your might and Your glory.

—Ps. 63:2–3

If I am to be guided by You, then You
must be present in my life, offering guidance. But so often I have no inkling, none
at all, of Your will for me. I lie in bed at
night wondering what You have in store
for me. Surely there must be more to my

life than this getting and spending, which occupies so much of my time and precious energy. Surely there is more: a unique purpose to my existence—some gift of my recovery that I am destined to share with others.

Indeed, there are moments when I have known fully why I am here. Whenever I tell the truth of my addiction and recovery, whenever I reach down to the pain I suffered and the pain I inflicted, whenever I listen to another's pain without judgment, then I know what my life is for. I am here to encourage others to feel, to grapple with and to tell their own truth. Whenever I support someone else's recovery, I feel Your presence supporting and enveloping me. Then I have no doubts. I am at one with what You will for me, Higher Power.

Is that all I need to know? That when I

am present for others, You will be present for me, showing me the way? Then I can turn the long stretches of famine into feasts. In return for Your truth, I offer You my praise.

Meeting in Silence

Only for God does my soul wait in
*   silence,*
for my deliverance is from God.
Only God is my rock, my deliverance,
my fortress; I shall not be shaken.

—Ps. 62:6–7

In silence, I listen to the sound of my breath. I hear myself inhale and watch my chest swell slightly; I hear the exhalation and watch my chest fall. I widen my mouth and nostrils to breathe more deeply. I see my chest and my belly filling up. I inhale and exhale slowly, breathing long and deep breaths.

As I fill up with each breath and listen to its quiet unvoiced sound, I think of the

first breath of life that came from God, the
Infinite Source of all being. I see and feel a
divine light moving, glowing in me. This,
then, is my soul. My soul and I are together
with God. We stay calm and peaceful for a
long time.

As my body becomes charged with the
energy of my soul, I know that my soul is a
reflection of Your cosmic soul. I contain a
spark of Your essence. As I feel Your grace
and love enveloping me, I intuit, Higher
Power, what You want from me today. My
mission is to bring peace to those around
me by being at peace within myself. May
serenity and well-being be my gifts to share
with others today and throughout my life.

Step Twelve

*H*aving had a spiritual awakening as a result of these steps,
we tried to carry this message
to others and to practice these
principles in all areas of our
lives.

Fellowship

We wandered in the wilderness,
lost our way in a wasteland,
never finding an inhabited place.
Hungry and thirsty,
we grew faint of spirit,
and in our distress, we cried to the
*   Deliverer;*
out of our straits God rescued us
and led us in a straight path
to an inhabited place.

—Ps. 107:4–7

I wandered in the desert of my addictions for many years, more than I would like to count. And I know that I'd be wandering there still had You not led me to a Twelve-Step fellowship, where I learned how to become honest with myself, with others and with You, Higher Power. Now that I'm abstinent from my addictive behaviors and becoming emotionally sober, the best thing I can do is praise You, Your Twelve Steps and their wisdom, which are a proven path for anyone suffering from addiction. The more I tell the story of my deliverance, the more I see that Yours is a spiritual cure for a spiritual dis-ease. It was my lack of self-love that propelled my addiction. Only You have been able to provide me with the constant assurance that I am loved for who I am.

When I reach a milestone in my recovery, I do not credit myself for my sobriety. It is by the grace of my Higher Power and the support of my fellowship that I have merited this moment of celebration. Such celebrations are important for everyone in the Twelve-Step rooms, for they provide hope for those of us still wandering, each in our separate desert, alone.

I am alone no longer. I enjoy my hours of solitude and my time with friends and family. I am constantly learning and growing through my partnership with You. For all the good that You have bestowed on me, Higher Power, I thank You. I will sing Your praises as long as I have breath to sing.

Carry This Message

I sought the Healer, who answered me
and saved me from all that I dread.
Those who look to You, God, become
*   radiant,*
and their faces do not look down in
*   shame.*
Comforter, You are near to the
*   brokenhearted,*
and those crushed in spirit You save.

—Ps. 34:5–6, 19

Coming into the rooms of my Twelve-Step fellowship, I was in excruciating pain. "Get it out. Get it out," they said to me. "Go to lots of meetings, open your mouth and share." And if I had not opened my mouth and cried out, I might still be active in my addiction—suffering silently, cut off from my feelings, and condemned by myself and by anyone else who knew of my addictive behavior.

But in the Twelve-Step rooms, I found compassion and acceptance. As I shared the pain of my broken heart and crushed spirit, You, Higher Power, did not spurn what I offered. Your answer came through those who reached out to support me, blessing me with their friendship, sharing their strength and hope in recovery. Gradually, I learned what it takes to listen to others. The more deeply I have listened, the more I have been able to reach out to those isolated in their own pain. As I did so, I lessened not only their isolation, but mine as well.

"It works if you work it, so work it, you're worth it," we say in our fellowship.

Each of us works our program differently, so there are many ways we carry the message. But carry it we must. If I do not share Your message with other addicts, I can easily become self-absorbed in my busy life and grow complacent about my recovery. Before I know it, I could be working on my relapse! So let me take care to spread this message and stay ever conscious, Higher Power, that I am doing Your work.

Practice These Principles

Who is the person who craves life,
desiring many years in which to see
good?
Guard your tongue from evil,
and your lips from speaking guile.
Turn from evil and do good;
Seek peace and pursue it.

—Ps. 34:13–15

Higher Power, let me take to heart the lessons of speech that I have learned in the Twelve-Step rooms. May I lose my impulse to gossip. May I refrain from speaking ill of other people. There will be far fewer hurt feelings to assuage or quarrels to mend. When someone annoys me, let me forget about that person's personality and focus instead on what I can learn about myself. Encourage me to be always kind and direct, pleasant and welcoming to all.

I would not have anyone but You stand in judgment over me. So teach me how not to judge others. As You see into other's hearts, so guide me toward greater empathy. And remind me that I can be most helpful to another when I discuss my own experience. May I do everything in my power to promote a safe and honest atmosphere for sharing, so healing and recovery may flourish.

We have been taught that "anonymity is the spiritual foundation of all our traditions." In protecting another's anonymity, we respect that person's right to privacy and dignity, just as we wish our privacy and dignity to be respected. Help me to remember that the confidences we share with one another are a sacred bond. It is You, not us, who brings the hidden to light, in Your time, not ours.

Grant me the wisdom, Higher Power, ever to put these principles into practice as I participate in the group life of our fellowship. Help me to draw people nearer to You, not push them away from Your path. May I love peace so much that I become a protector of the peace within our rooms. For it is indeed good when brothers and sisters in recovery sit down in loving fellowship together.

What God Promises

Kindness and truth shall meet;
justice and peace shall kiss.
Truth shall sprout from the earth,
and righteousness look down from
*　　heaven.*
You, Provider, shall surely grant all that
*　　is good,*
and our land bring forth its produce.
Justice shall go before You,
making a path for Your footsteps.

　　　　　　　　　　　　—Ps. 85:11–14

Addiction is first and foremost a dis-ease of the soul. I came into recovery so alienated from You, Higher Power, and so removed from the best in myself that I could no longer survive in the life I was leading. You have restored me beyond my imagining, to a sane, satisfying and productive life. The seeds that I planted in tears have yielded an abundant harvest of joy and inner peace. My peace of mind is at risk, however, when other addicts suffer and I do nothing to lessen their suffering. So inspire me, Higher Power, to share my joy in recovery with those who still suffer from this dis-ease.

The joy I know today is rooted in Your love and caring. As I have been cared for by You and by others in my fellowship, I have learned how to truly care for myself and for others. Walking the Twelve-Step path, I have seen that we are not just recovering individuals, but a recovering community, who influence one another for good and for ill. Help me to remember that my recovery has a ripple effect on the world. As I continue making amends to those I wronged through my addiction, I do my part to bring justice and healing where there was pain and harm. As I grow in recovery, I am learning to treat others with the same respect and love with which I want to be treated. As I am truthful and continue to own responsibility for my actions, justice and peace with others becomes possible in all areas of my life.

Through all this miraculous growth, I have come face to face with an astounding truth. Through my relationship with You, Higher Power, my deepest needs are being met. As I look around me, I see how far the world is from recognizing that simple truth. People are in desperate need not only of jobs, food, clothing, shelter and medical care, but also in need of the spiritual sustenance You so amply provide. As I have been sustained by Your soul food, so teach me to share it with others. Show me how I can work for a world in which everyone's deepest needs will be met. Help me to see how I can spread kindness and truth, justice and peace to all. May this be Your will.

A Note on the Translations

In preparing the adaptation of these passages from the Psalms, I have consulted the original Hebrew as well as Christian and Jewish versions of the Bible in English. Verse numbers refer to the Jewish Bible, which in some cases vary slightly from standard Christian texts. I have generally chosen to recast as direct address ("You, God") those passages that describe God in the third person ("He"). I hope this allows readers the intimacy of addressing God directly and the freedom of not having to assign a gender to their Higher Power. In one case, I have shifted a pronoun from "they" to "we," in order to speak more directly to the recovering community.

In calling on the One to whom these prayers are addressed, I use a variety of names, as is the practice in all the monotheistic religions. These names draw upon the context of each psalm to evoke numerous attributes of the divine. For example, the most familiar English address to God, "Lord," is itself an approximation. It does not translate the most sacred biblical name for God, but rather the term "Adonai," which Jews substitute in prayer for the unpronounceable name, "YHVH." (That name has sometimes been vocalized as Jehovah or Yahweh; a remnant survives in the phrase Hallelu-YAH!, meaning "Praise YAH!"). YAH and YHVH are derived from the Hebrew verb "to be." The most appropriate translation might therefore be "The One Who Is, Was and Will Be." Calling God the Eternal or the Ever-Present captures for me the basic meaning of this all-important name. An index of these various terms follows so readers can explore how different names resonate with their own needs and moods.

THREE GUIDES
FOR USING THIS BOOK

Topics

Names of God

Psalms Cited

Healing Leaves

Reb Noson's letters, based on the understanding and love he learned from the great chassidic master, Rebbe Nachman of Breslov, show how each of us can find strength and confidence to renew our lives in a positive and meaningful way.

The main thing is for you to have the belief in yourself, like my belief in you, that you can still make a new start now.

From the letters of
Reb Noson of Breslov
(1780–1844)

Code #7656 • Quality Paperback • $7.95

Fiction from Simcha Press
The Promise of God

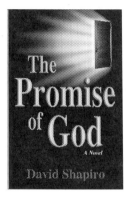

What if: the word of God suddenly echoed from the drug-ridden cities of South America; the world's most prominent media mogul became personally consumed with the quest for world peace; powerful forces in the universe seemed to be drawing toward an unavoidable and monumental collision? This exciting adventure will take you around the world and keep you on the edge of your seat as the set-up for final eradication of anti-Semitism.

Code #7443 • Quality Paperback • $12.95

New Age Judaism

Many people will be sur-
prised to find that Judaism
is fundamentally aligned
with what we think of as
the New Age. Many of
the things we associate
with the New Age are
not new but are part of
Kabbalah, the Jewish
mystical tradition. *New
Age Judaism* is not about
Judaism modified to meet

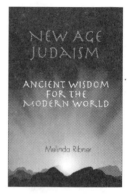

the needs of the moment, but rather it makes age-
old Judaism, traditional and kabbalistic teachings
accessible to the modern person in a new way.

Code #7893 • Quality Paperback • $9.95